Christmas Grace
Created By:
Nichole Radecki

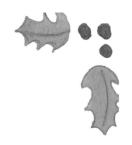

To my loving family and wonderful husband, Ryan. Thank you for all your love and support! God Bless!

1 Corinthians 13:4-5 NIV

Love is patient, love is kind. It does not envy, it does not boast, it is not proud. It does not dishonor others, it is not self-seeking, it is not easily angered, it keeps no record of wrongs.

Christmas

Grace

Christmas time is
coming soon,
all the children
sang a tune.

They hung their stockings nice and
high,
while mom was baking a
Christmas pie.

Their hearts were happy, full of joy, praying for Santa to bring them lots of toys.

The Christmas tree shone
nice and bright,
their whole front yard was
filled with lights.

But in the corner
Steven hid,
plotting evil against
his brother Sid.

Steven was mean, bad
to the core,
all the stockings he soon
tore.

His mother saw what he
had done,
and Steven was to have
no more fun.

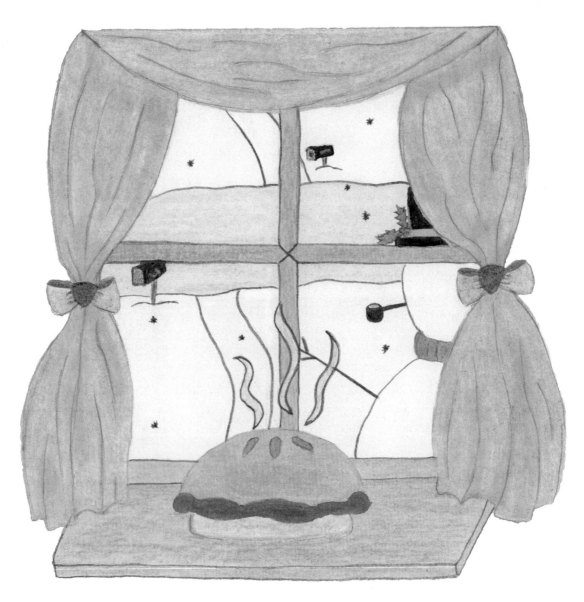

She sent him straight
to bed,
no Christmas pie he
was fed.

Christmas morning finally came,
all the children were ready
to play some games.

The children's new
stockings all nice and full,
only one was filled high
with coal.

As tears ran down
Steven's eyes,
a crooked little smile
told him otherwise.

For in Sid's paws
he held out a toy,
and in Steven's heart
he knew he was a
good boy.

"But why?" He asked, "for I've been nothing but naughty."
Sid soon explained, "but I know you are sorry."

THE END

About the Author

Nichole Radecki is 25 years old and received a Bachelor's Degree in Environmental Biology from Ohio University. She currently lives in Columbus, Ohio where she enjoys being active with her husband by hiking, running, and biking on the beautiful trails. She also loves writing and drawing in her free time and inspiring others.